I0494727

VIRTUAL PRESENTATIONS MADE SIMPLE

Practical tips for effective web presentations

. . .

Colette Johnson

Copyright © 2016 Colette Johnson
ALL RIGHTS RESERVED

ISBN: 1537013904
ISBN-13: 978-1537013909

Without limiting the rights under copyright reserved above, no part of this publication may be reproduced, stored in or introduced into a retrieval system, or transmitted, in any form, or by any means (electronic, mechanical, photocopying, recording, or otherwise), without the prior contractual or written permission of the copyright owner of this work.

.   .   .   .   .

Cover, Layout and eBook by
N.D. Author Services [NDAS]
www.NDAuthorServices.com

Contents

Introduction

Virtual presentations are becoming standard practice for businesses needing to save time and money. There is no doubt that they can be much more time efficient and save small fortunes on travel and hotel costs but are they necessarily more effective? More productive? The answer is that they can be—with the right preparation, knowledge and structure. And that's where this book comes in handy. Follow these tips and you will be able to confidently prepare, structure and deliver a truly effective virtual presentation.

Firstly let's clarify for the purposes of this book what we mean by 'virtual presentations':

A web-based presentation using a platform such as Adobe Connect, Go To Webinar/Go To Meeting, Webex, Skype.

A virtual presentation may include the following elements:

- Audio conferencing via PC, laptop, phone or mobile device
- Webcams

- Visuals e.g. slides, documents
- Audience interaction

Who should read this book?

This book will be a valuable guide if you are...

- ✔ New to any kind of presenting
- ✔ An experienced face to face presenter but less experienced virtual presenter
- ✔ Lacking in confidence when addressing a group
- ✔ Conducting online meetings, sales pitches, product demo's or webinars
- ✔ In need of structure for your virtual presentations
- ✔ Looking for ways to make your virtual presentations more engaging, interesting and stimulating

It is likely that the intended audience for your presentation is geographically spread and therefore a face to face presentation may be impractical with regards to time, location and cost.

A virtual presentation should never be seen as a less desirable option to a face to face presentation. In fact it can be more engaging, more impactful and more effective when delivered in the right way.

What will you learn in this book?

This book is not intended to be a guide for online presentation technology. It advances so quickly that many of the functions would be out of date by the time the book was published!

The overall aim of this book is to equip you with some useful and practical tips that will help you prepare, structure and deliver successful virtual presentations with confidence.

You will learn how to:

1. Prepare effectively
2. Take control at the start of your presentation
3. Keep on track throughout
4. Generate and maintain interest
5. Use your body language to maximum effect, even when your audience cannot see you
6. Engage the audience through your tone of voice and the words you use
7. Encourage your audience to interact
8. Decide when to speak and when to listen
9. Link smoothly from one visual to the next
10. Start and end your presentation with impact
11. Handle questions effectively
12. Be a confident and professional virtual presenter

Before Your Presentation

Tip 1: Understand the virtual medium

Presenting virtually is a very different dynamic from a face to face presentation. The main points to bear in mind are:

- The majority of the population is highly visual. As your audience cannot see you there needs to be lots of stimulating visuals in your presentation to maintain their interest
- Attention spans are waning across the population as a whole. According to 'Statistic Brain' the average attention span in 2000 was 12 seconds, compared with just 8.35 seconds in 2015. Attention spans online are shorter than in the physical meeting room as there are more distractions to disengage your

audience e.g. computer screens, mobile phones, other people. This means you have to prepare ways of engaging and keeping your audience's attention (see tip 12)

- The slides you use in a face to face presentation will not necessarily work well in a virtual presentation (see tip 18 for information on visuals) so use a different set of visuals for your virtual presentations
- You will need to use your voice tone differently when delivering a virtual presentation. (see tip 17)
- Your messages should be more concise than in a physical environment, less 'wordy' and crystal clear
- Things happen more quickly in a virtual presentation than face to face. The whole experience is condensed and much faster paced. Learn to respond quickly and get to the point
- Body language makes a difference. Even though your audience cannot see you, your body language will affect the way you sound (see tip 21)
- Never underestimate how much time it takes to prepare a virtual presentation (or indeed, any presentation at all)

- Time can run away with you in a virtual presentation, especially if technical issues arise. Always allocate longer than you think you will need. People generally won't mind at all if you finish ahead of time but they may be inconvenienced if you over-run
- Things can and do go wrong in the virtual world. Often this is outside your control, for example poor connectivity. The more prepared you are the better you are able to cope with unexpected situations. Confidence is the key—you may not be able to affect what happens but you can affect how you deal with it
- Invest in a quality headset with good sound quality
- Make sure you are seated in a comfortable position and that your chair does not make distracting squeaks or creaks!
- Turn off your email alerts

Tip 2: Do the groundwork

The administration side of your virtual presentation is the detail that often gets overlooked or skimped on. It is important to spend some time thinking about who should attend, what they may need beforehand and whether the timing of your presentation is suitable for all attendees, especially if spread across the globe.

Send out joining instructions at least two weeks ahead of your presentation. To make sure the timing works across any relevant time zones www.timeanddate.com has a useful meeting planner tool that can help you coordinate time zones in different parts of the world.

Together with calendar invites it's also useful to send an agenda for your presentation and let the audience know what they are likely to gain from attending.

In addition, you may want to send supplementary information with your invite such as a video link, documents or a questionnaire.

Tip 3: Find out about your audience

Ideally your research will result in you finding out:

- How many people will be in your audience? You might be presenting to many more people than you think. Audience members often share their screens or conference phones
- What they do (job roles/ status)
- How much they know about your subject already
- What their expectations are of the presentation—i.e. are they expecting it to be formal or informal / one way or interactive
- What your audience's business needs are i.e. what problem is your presentation designed to solve? This is particularly important in a sales presentation
- What they want to achieve from the presentation e.g. what outcome they are expecting
- Different cultures—this impacts on your audience's expectations and also on how they interact during the presentation

People in your organisation who may have had dealings with your audience members are often useful points of reference when doing your research. LinkedIn is also a useful source of information.

Tip 4: Define your purpose

Without a clear purpose your presentation will be aimless and woolly. After all, *'A man who is going nowhere usually gets there'*.

Getting clarity on your overall purpose is vital because everything you say or do in your presentation needs to align with your purpose. This will convey authenticity and authority to your audience and generally add strength to your message.

Asking yourself the following questions will help you define your purpose:

1. What is the overall message I want my audience to go away with?

> This helps you identify one clear objective for your presentation and keeps you on track

2. What's in it for them?

> This is crucial because it helps you to deliver a presentation that benefits the audience. If you can show that you understand a problem that your audience has, and then go on to provide a solution to it, your presentation will be a hit.

3. How do I want my audience to feel at the end of my presentation?

A point that's often missed and yet it's so important. Our audience's emotions are, to a certain extent, within our sphere of influence. If you want your audience to feel motivated you need to be motivational. If you want them to feel reassured you need to use reassuring language and an empathic tone of voice... and so on.

4. What action(s) do I want my audience to take as a result of my presentation?

Working towards and ending with a 'call to action' tells your audience what you want them to do next. You may want them to book a product demonstration, progress a buying decision to the next stage or even place an order there and then

Tip 5: Learn the technical stuff

When a virtual presentation goes wrong it is almost never to do with the presenter or the content of their presentation. When problems occur it's usually the technical side of things that can jeopardise your presentation.

Whatever platform you choose to use for your presentation it's advisable to do an online tutorial or take a look at the user guidelines. They will take you through the basic 'how-to's' and help build your knowledge and confidence with the system.

If using a new environment for your virtual presentation always check the connectivity out and have a practice run. Technology in your own home or a hotel room may be far inferior to the system in your office.

Once you are familiar with the system always practice using the features and functions that you will be using in your presentation. Rehearse the words you will use to link from one visual to another and check all weblinks and videos are working properly.

Tip 6: Be creative with functions and features

Different virtual platforms have varying features but most of them enable the presenter to:

- Make someone else a presenter (meaning that they will be able to share a document or screen with the group)
- Send and receive live messages in the chat box
- Run polls
- See a list of participants
- Hear a sound whenever someone joins or leaves the virtual meeting room
- Share documents / screens
- Ask participants to use emoticons to interact, eg raise a hand, show a smiley face, thumbs up/down
- Show video clips

Some systems also allow the presenter to split the audience into smaller groups and work in 'breakout rooms' where they share ideas and write on individual whiteboards which can then be shared with the larger group.

Learn the functions available to you and then use them to add variety and interest to your presentation.

Tip 7: Structure your presentation

Essentially your presentation needs to have a clear beginning, middle and end:

Opening	Ground rules, introductions, setting expectations for the presentation
Middle	Key messages supported by visuals, examples, stories, polls, chat
End	Summary, questions and answers, call to action

A good way to put your presentation together is to start by listing all the key points you wish to make and write them each on individual sticky notes. Then put them into a logical order and remove any duplicate messages. Once you are happy with the order, decide on the visuals you will use that can add value to your messages.

Start with your messages and not with the visuals, otherwise there is a danger that your presentation is simply a deck of pretty slides that do not necessarily align with your overall purpose.

Many people find it helpful to script their virtual presentation. What I mean by this is to type out what you are going to say, the links from one visual to another, and when/where to use polls, share documents etc.

This will give you confidence and help you to rehearse. Do make sure that you practice to the point where you can make it sound natural—there is nothing worse than someone sounding as if they are reading from a script.

Checklist for preparing your virtual presentation

Preparation step	√ / x
Joining instructions sent	
Audience researched	
Purpose defined	
Technical features/functions learnt and practiced	
Key messages created	
Visuals designed	
Polls created	
Opening scripted and practiced	
Case studies / testimonials prepared	
Expected questions thought through and answers rehearsed	
Closing statement written	

During Your Presentation

Tip 8: Open your presentation and set the scene

It's vitally important to get the start of a virtual presentation right. The beginning can be chaotic with people unable to join the meeting room/call, others joining late and interrupting the flow, any number of technical issues, not to mention dogs barking in the background!

Always make sure you can join the virtual meeting room / call at least 15 minutes before the start, in case of technical issues. Get your handouts and documents loaded ready to share and make sure all web links are working.

Type a welcome message into the chat box before you start and also the dial-in number for joining by conference call (if applicable). This is helpful to people who have joined the virtual meeting room but may be having dial-in problems.

Check your participant list to see who is joining and who is yet to join. My advice is to start on time provided most of your participants have logged in.

Following The 'GRADE' acronym will help you to cover the essentials at the opening stage of your presentation:

Greeting and Ground rules

Your name, job title and if necessary briefly give any background information that supports your authority to present the subject, e.g. experience, results achieved. If appropriate, ask all participants to introduce themselves. Ask the audience to mute their microphones if in a noisy office; shut down any devices not being used for this call; ask them to state their name first before speaking, e.g. *'John here, can I just ask....'*

Explain how the technology works, e.g. how to unmute microphones; when to use the chat box and where emoticons can be found.

At this point it is good practice to check if there are other people in the audience who are not on the participant list

Reason

State the reason for the presentation. Show understanding of the audience's needs, problems and if appropriate, concerns. Explain that you will be addressing their needs.

Agenda

Explain what will be covered—keep it to 3 main subject areas so that people can easily follow it

Duration/ Detail

State how long the presentation will last, tell them when questions are invited and whether handouts will be supplied.

End goals

Explain what the audience will think, feel or do differently as a result of your presentation. Imagine they are thinking 'what's in it for me?' Make a statement that answers these questions and tell the audience the benefits they will reap from attending your presentation. Start with *'By the end of this presentation you will...'*

Example presentation opening using GRADE

Greeting

Hello everyone, my name is xxxxx and I am (job role) at (your company name) Thank you for inviting us to talk to you today to introduce our company and (product/service name) to you

I'm aware that some of you don't know each other so let's start by introducing ourselves. James, can you start please by telling everyone your role and responsibilities?

Ground rules

A few reminders to ensure everything goes smoothly—please can everyone make sure all devices are switched off apart from those you may be using to connect right now! Please do use your microphones to speak whenever you wish but I would ask that otherwise you keep them on mute if you are in a noisy office.

Let's just make sure we're all familiar with the features we'll be using in this session (emoticons/chat)...

Finally, when you do address the group please say your name before speaking so that we can identify you.

Reason

We understand that you currently use x system, which you have told us is time con-

suming and costly. You are looking to enhance this system without too much upheaval and to reduce costs and save time. Today we aim to show you how we can help you achieve this.

Agenda

During this presentation we will cover: How our product can integrate with your existing system seamlessly, the return on investment you can expect, and next steps to making it happen

Duration

We will spend 30 minutes with you today and take questions as we go through. Additional information will be sent to you by 5pm today

End goals

By the end of this presentation you will see how (company name) can work with you to help you meet your budget and timesaving targets and how we can add value to your organisation

Tip 9: Start with a powerful message

Begin your presentation with an attention-grabbing statement or question that makes your audience sit up and listen to you. Your opening message will set the tone for the rest of your presentation so make sure it creates a positive impact.

Here are some ideas for your opening point:

1. An interesting or shocking fact/ statistic
2. A quotation from a famous person or from someone in your organisation
3. A short relevant video clip or soundbite
4. A question (ask for a show of hands from the audience)

Tip 10: Play music

There can be awkward moments before the start of your presentation when people are joining the virtual meeting room and nobody is speaking. Music can set the tone for your presentation and create the right mood and playing music at this point can be very effect- ive, provided you choose the right track. For example, Vivaldi's 'Four Seasons' is both up- lifting and easy to listen to. There may be a piece of music that is relevant to your presentation subject—this can work well but take care that you don't cross over into cheesiness!

Some virtual platforms have a music facility built in but if not, just play music through your computer. Do check the volume is ac- ceptable for participants though.

Tip 11: Use a webcam at the start

If using a webcam I suggest switching it on at the start of the presentation for your intro-duction. This helps to personalise the experi-ence and demonstrates that you are a real person, not just an anonymous voice. After your introduction turn off your webcam and focus on your delivery. This ensures that your audience focusses on content rather than on you the presenter.

Tip 12: Engage the audience

An online presentation needs to be more interactive and fast paced than a face to face presentation. There are many distractions when online from emails to more interesting things going on outside the office window. Your job as an online presenter is to engage the audience and make them want to hear what you have to say.

With a smaller group (e.g. up to 15 people) it is advisable to get interaction verbally from the audience by asking them to use their microphones and speak to you. It is etiquette for people to mute their microphones, however, when in a noisy environment that may be distracting for the rest of the group.

Some virtual platforms enable the presenter to see a participation chart for each audience member, to track who is interacting and who hasn't spoken or typed anything for x number of minutes. This can be really helpful for a virtual training session where every participant is expected to interact.

Here are some ideas for encouraging interaction in your virtual presentation:

- Use polls—these are a quick and easy way to find out what your audience thinks

- Ask questions and select specific people to answer them (remember to get them to unmute their microphone first)
- Ask a question and ask people to write their answers into the chat box
- Relate to your audience members by name: 'Sue, I know you were particularly interested in how this impacts on your team….' Clearly this is only workable if your audience is relatively small. In a larger group, however, it is still possible to refer to people by name when they have written in the chat box. For example, "Greg, I think everyone can relate to the point you've just made……" and then share Greg's point with the group
- If your presentation involves doing a product demo, get your audience to have a go—let them practice using the system and help them through it
- Play a relevant video clip and ask for feedback afterwards
- Ask feedback questions: 'How does this idea sound to you, Jan?' / How does that *fit in with your current system, Raj?*'

Poll example

Q: What is your key priority in Q3?	
Talent management	
New product launch	
Customer service	

With a poll, participants click on their chosen option and results will show immediately on your screen in the form of a bar graph. You can also select to see individual responses if you wish.

Example probing questions

- *Andreus, **how** does Freda's suggestion fit with your department?*
- *Annelise, **where** do you see Raj's idea working within your project?*
- *Cathy, **who** in your department could use that idea?*

Questions to elicit feedback

- Hardeep, you've been a little quiet, what are your thoughts so far?
- *Anya, **who** has said something so far that you can really relate to?*
- *Lucy, **what** has struck a chord with you in the call so far?*

Questions to test understanding

1. *Linda, could you please summarise what has been said about.......*
- *Tomasz, what's your understanding of.......*
- *Mo, would you please recap on the key points covered so far....*

As a general rule, the presenter should aim to speak for no more than five minutes at a time before getting interaction (physical or verbal) from the audience.

Tip 13: Tell your story

Storytelling can be a highly effective way to get your messages across, especially when accompanied by appropriate visuals. Stories can capture our imaginations and change the way people act, think and feel. Consider using allegories, metaphors, real 'stories' from your own business or industry to liven up your presentation and add interest.

I can recommend 'TED Talks Storytelling' by Akash Karia for storytelling ideas and techniques.

Tip 14: Relate to your audience

Your audience will be more engaged if they feel that you are speaking directly to them, relating to their own feelings, thoughts and experiences. This can be achieved by person-alising your messages rather than stating them in a remote and factual way.

For example, instead of saying *'These are the ways you can use our system'*, You could describe (and show visuals of) 'Paul in Order Processing', 'Freda in Payroll', and demon-strate how they use your systems in their departments. This is a simple and very effect-ive tool that engages people and makes your ideas more accessible to them.

Tip 15: Mind your language

When you were preparing your presentation you thought about how you wanted your audience to feel at the end (or at least you did if you paid attention to tip 4!). Your words and phrases need to align with this i.e. if you want your audience to feel motivated by your presentation you need to use motivational language—maybe include some inspiring quotes or examples / stories.

Virtual presenters often make the mistake of saying too much. This is usually because when we are nervous we tend to ramble and not being able to see or 'read' your audience can make the presenter nervous.

Listening is an essential part of presenting —don't be afraid to ask a question and use the power of the pause to encourage your audience to open up and share their views.

Nerves can also result in indecisive and 'woolly language e.g. 'Hopefully', 'Possibly', 'Just'....

Scripting can help you to use positive language and practice helps it stick.

Language to use in your presentation:

1. **Repetition**—use the power of 3 (see next tip) and repeat important points 3 times
2. **Audience member's names**—helps to them keep engaged
3. **Alliteration**—adds interest and aids retention e.g. 'Product, Price, Promotion'
4. **Acronyms**—e.g. 'GRADE'
5. **'Because'**—it satisfies the audience's need for more information

Linking from one message or slide to the next

Beware that you don't fall into the trap of repeating *'and the next slide shows...'* throughout your presentation. Not all of your slides will need introducing. Your slides and images are there to support your narrative, rather than the other way around.

Here are some phrases you can use to add variety to link your messages and slides:

1. *As you can see here....*
2. *Which brings us to...*
3. *Let's look at how that works...*
4. *Focussing now on the detail...*
5. *Moving on now to.....*

Tip 16: Use the power of three

There are numerous examples from the natural, mathematical, art, music and theological worlds as to why three is a magical and powerful number. In business we know when we use the power of three we help people register and retain information quickly and easily.

In your virtual presentation the power of three can be used to:

1. Outline what you will be covering (your agenda)
2. Focus on three key messages in the main body of your presentation
3. Repeat an important point (3 times)
4. Give three possible answers in a poll question
5. Structure your presentation (opening, middle and end)

Tip 17: Speak with impact

When sitting or standing in a room and addressing a group of people you need to project your voice a considerable amount. In a virtual presentation it is not necessary to speak loudly but it is very important to use your voice effectively to engage your audience and maintain their interest.

Here are some tips for speaking with impact when presenting online:

- **Smile!** Even though your audience can't see you they can hear your smile. Fortunately they don't know whether or not it is genuine. So even if you are shaking with nerves, forcing yourself to smile will result in your audience responding positively toward you
- **Slow down**—practice speaking more slowly than is comfortable. When face to face we lip read an awful lot and you don't have that advantage in a virtual presentation. So slow down, let your audience absorb your message and then move on
- **Vary your pitch**—we all have the ability to lower or raise the pitch of our voice but often we fall into a

comfortable monotone that can bore an audience to tears. Record yourself speaking and give yourself a critical appraisal. Does your voice come across as too high? Too low? Too varied? Not varied enough? Beware the rising inflection—this is where the end of the sentence goes up as if asking a question. This can make you seem unsure of your message. A falling inflection (going down at the end of the sentence) makes you sound more assertive

Tip 18: Keep interest high with strong visuals

A variety of visuals helps your audience engage with your messages e.g. PowerPoint slides (or Prezi), documents, video.

Visuals should be clear, concise and add value to your message. Here are some tips for creating great visuals:

- Make visuals more simple and images bigger than in a face to face presentation
- Use bright colours to gain attention and stimulate the senses. You only have two senses at your disposal, sight and sound, so it stands to reason that you need to make the most of them
- Put one message on each slide
- Focus on pictures and graphics rather than words
- Use charts, graphs, images that are easy to read and understand—anything over-complicated will lose the audience quickly
- Use more slides than you would face to face. On average one slide every 2-3 minutes online is a good rule to follow

- Avoid reading your slides
- Avoid slides with bullet points. They are boring, predictable and not very creative

www.slideshare.net is a good starting point for visuals—be selective as there are some shockers on there, but search around and you will get some ideas.

Tip 19: Demonstrate credibility

One of the most powerful influencers is social proof. Your audience want to know what you have done before that's worked, proof of who you have worked with and results achieved.

Case studies and testimonials can be really effective, particularly quick 20 second sound-bites from satisfied customers which you can capture and play back on short video clips

Tip 20: Be a problem solver

Think about how you can make life easier for your audience—perhaps your product or service can save them time, money, hassle? Demonstrate an understanding of your audience's problems and what solutions you can offer e.g. *"You've told us that it takes a long time to retrieve data using your current system. We can reduce that retrieval time by 75% with this product"*

Tip 21: Sit up and pay attention

Body language really does make a difference even when you can't see your audience. Of course you may be using a webcam for your introduction in which case you need to be aware of your 'screensaver face' i.e. the expression your face defaults to when you're not consciously doing anything with it. Your tongue-out concentration face may not help your professional image!

Make sure you sit up straight when presenting—a slouched posture will cause your lungs to constrict and your voice to sound 'squashed', and a smile (see tip 14) will work wonders.

Tip 22: Handle questions with confidence

Questions can arise at any stage of your presentation and really should be welcomed rather than dreaded. If you are presenting to a large audience you may prefer to ask the audience to type their questions into the chat box and then you can select which ones you answer. This enables you to manage your time efficiently.

With a smaller group (up to 15 people) questions can be asked verbally using participant's microphones. This is preferable as you get immediate feedback and can relate directly to the questioner.

When answering questions:

- Thank the questioner
- Clarify your understanding of the question where necessary by repeating it back
- Answer the question concisely or say you will get back to them with the answer
- Check they are happy with the answer

With any leftover questions in the chat box you can email the answers to the whole group after the presentation.

Ending Your Presentation

Tip 23: End with a bang, not a whimper

Once you have covered your key messages summarise them (using the power of three), answer any final questions and then close your presentation. Your closing statement or question could be a call to action—aligned with what you want your audience to think or do differently at the end of your presentation.

For example you could:

- Invite the audience to a demonstration of your product/service
- Assume they are going ahead with the next stage of the process
- Ask for their support for a proposal

Your ending needs to have a positive impact and a clear intention.

Tip 24: Rehearse, rehearse and rehearse again

By rehearsing I mean deliver your presentation out loud, practicing with the virtual technology that you will be using for the real thing. Don't take anything for granted—the little things can trip you up if you don't think them through beforehand. Work with your script and try it out on a willing volunteer. Make sure you know how to switch from one screen or function to another, practice running a poll and sharing the results, share a document and run through your slides.

Once you have rehearsed your presentation a few times you will be more confident about timing. It's very easy to underestimate how long a virtual presentation takes, especially when your audience is interacting throughout.

Tip 25: Keep improving

We are our own worst critic. Be objective about your virtual presenting skills and learn from what works and what doesn't. Most on-line platforms have a recording facility—this is useful for watching/hearing yourself back and assessing your skills.

Here is a self-assessment checklist to use after each presentation:

Element of presentation	Comments
Greeting / Ground rules	
Reason for presentation	
Agenda	
Duration / Detail	
Clear, bold visuals	
End goals	
Voice clarity/pitch /pace	
Clear, concise messages	
Powerful language	
Handle questions confidently	
Close with a call to action	

About
Colette Johnson

Colette Johnson is re-
cognised as a top Sales
and Presentation Skills
Trainer.

Since 1993 she has
built up a wealth of ex-
perience designing and
delivering training pro-
grammes for organi-
sations across Europe,
helping them develop
their sales skills and win more business.

Colette's clients are increasingly using virtual platforms to communicate with their
internal and external customers and are finding that the virtual medium brings its own
unique set of challenges. Colette's company
Simply Sales Training is responding to that
need with tailored training courses in both
face to face and virtual presentation skills.

With many clients wanting advice on
presenting virtually, Colette decided to collate
her experiences and tips into this simple and
practical guide. To contact Colette:

Colette@simplysalestraining.co.uk
www.simplysalestraining.co.uk
Tel: +44 (118) 987 5683